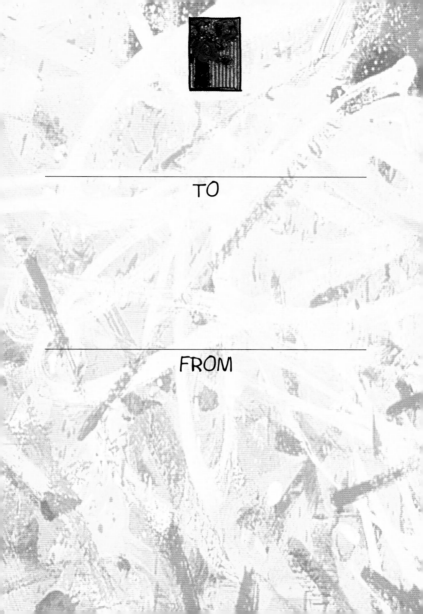

TO

FROM

SPECIAL DAYS

SEND ME FLYING

ON YOUR SPECIAL DAY

DON'T WAIT

TO CELEBRATE.
I'VE DECLARED IT
"NATIONAL CELEBRATE
YOU" DAY!

IF I WERE

TO MAKE A SOLEMN
SPEECH IN PRAISE
OF YOU, IN
GRATITUDE,
IN DEEP
AFFECTION,
YOU WOULD
TURN AN
ALARMING
SHADE OF
CRIMSON
AND TRY
TO ESCAPE.
SO I WON'T.
TAKE IT
ALL AS SAID.

Marion Garretty

Don't Look Now

CONGRATULATIONS! YOU'RE
A STAR. I ALWAYS KNEW
THAT YOU'D GO FAR!

Michelle Samara

THESE THINGS I WARMLY
WISH FOR YOU—
A DAY TO CELEBRATE
AND DREAMS COME TRUE,
A LITTLE SUN,
A BIT OF CHEER
AND SPECIAL FRIENDS
ALWAYS NEAR.

LET THE CONFETTI FLY AND THE STREAMERS UNFURL. BRING ON THE CAKE—IT'S TIME TO CELEBRATE!

FORGET THE CAKE. GO FOR THE ICING!

SOMEWHERE ON THE
GREAT WORLD THE SUN
IS ALWAYS SHINING....
THERE IS SO MUCH
SUNSHINE WE MUST ALL
HAVE OUR SHARE.

Myrtle Reed

EVERYONE HAS HIS DAY
AND SOME DAYS LAST
LONGER THAN OTHERS.

Winston Churchill

THE DIFFERENCE BETWEEN
THE ORDINARY AND THE
EXTRAORDINARY IS THAT
LITTLE EXTRA. AND YOU'RE
EXTRAORDINARY!

NEVER FORGET THAT LIFE
IS SPECIAL. EVERY SINGLE
DAY IS A SPECIAL DAY.

Charles R. Swindoll

LIFE IS A GREAT BIG
CANVAS, AND YOU SHOULD
THROW ALL THE PAINT
ON IT YOU CAN.

Danny Kaye

REAL FRIENDS ARE THOSE WHO, WHEN YOU'VE MADE A FOOL OF YOURSELF, DON'T FEEL AS THOUGH YOU'VE DONE A PERMANENT JOB.

SO, RATHER THAN APPEAR FOOLISH AFTERWARD, I RENOUNCE SEEMING CLEVER NOW.

William of Baskerville

To Every Dog There Is A Season: Spring

LAUGHTER

IS A NOISY SMILE!

Steven Goldberg

AMBITION...CREATES
DISENCHANTMENT WITH
THE ORDINARY AND PUTS
THE DARE INTO DREAMS.

Max Lucado

16

THERE IS NOTHING LIKE A
DREAM TO CREATE THE
FUTURE.

Victor Hugo

DREAMS COME A SIZE
TOO BIG SO THAT WE
CAN GROW INTO THEM.

Josie Bisset

LOOK BACKWARD WITH
GRATITUDE AND FORWARD
TO ALL THE CELEBRATIONS
YET TO COME.

IT IS MORE BLESSED TO
GIVE THAN TO RECEIVE.

The Book of Acts

A LITTLE NONSENSE NOW
AND THEN IS RELISHED BY
THE BEST OF MEN.

HAPPINESS IS SOMETHING
THAT COMES INTO OUR
LIVES THROUGH A DOOR
WE DON'T REMEMBER
LEAVING OPEN.

BE GLAD OF LIFE BECAUSE
IT GIVES YOU A CHANCE
TO LOVE AND TO WORK
AND TO PLAY AND TO
LOOK UP AT THE STARS.

Henry Van Dyke

MAY ONLY GOOD THINGS
COME YOUR WAY
EVERY MOMENT OF TODAY.

HE HAS MADE EVERYTHING
BEAUTIFUL IN ITS TIME.

The Book of Ecclesiastes

THIS TIME, LIKE ALL
OTHER TIMES, IS A
VERY GOOD ONE, IF WE
BUT KNOW WHAT TO DO
WITH IT.

Ralph Waldo Emerson

As The Sun Sets Slowly In The West, We Bid You A Fine Farewell

I'M AN

IDEALIST. I DON'T KNOW
WHERE I'M GOING, BUT
I'M ON MY WAY.

Carl Sandburg

A FRIEND IS A PERSON
WITH A SNEAKY KNACK
OF SAYING GOOD THINGS
ABOUT YOU BEHIND
YOUR BACK.

TO GET THE FULL
VALUE OF JOY YOU
MUST HAVE SOMEONE
TO DIVIDE IT WITH.

Mark Twain

LOOKING FORWARD TO
THINGS IS HALF THE
PLEASURE OF THEM.

Lucy Maud Montgomery

WE WERE CREATED WITH
AN OVERWHELMING DESIRE
TO SOAR...REALISTICALLY
DREAMING OF WHAT GOD
CAN DO WITH OUR
POTENTIAL.

Carol Kent

HAPPINESS IS A FRIEND
WHO PULLS THE TOILET
PAPER OFF YOUR SHOE
BEFORE YOU MAKE YOUR
GRAND ENTRANCE.

GOD GAVE ME FRIENDS SO
THAT I WOULDN'T HAVE
TO LAUGH ALONE.

THE WORLD IS FULL OF
ALL KINDS OF JOY, BUT
IT'S SPECIAL PEOPLE LIKE
YOU WHO MAKE THE
NICEST KIND.

LOOK FOR THE HEAVEN
HERE ON EARTH. IT IS
ALL AROUND YOU.

LIVE YOUR LIFE WHILE YOU
HAVE IT. LIFE IS A
SPLENDID GIFT—THERE IS
NOTHING SMALL ABOUT IT.

Florence Nightingale

WRITE ON YOUR HEART
THAT EVERY DAY IS THE
BEST DAY OF THE YEAR.

Ralph Waldo Emerson

WE DO NOT REMEMBER
DAYS, WE REMEMBER
MOMENTS. MAKE MOMENTS
WORTH REMEMBERING.

Hair Club For Dogs

WHEN

OTHERS ARE HAPPY,

BE HAPPY WITH THEM.

The Book of Romans

LAUGH AT YOURSELF,
BEFORE ANYONE ELSE CAN.

Elsa Maxwell

A LIGHT HEART LIVES
LONG.

Shakespeare

EVERY PERSON'S LIFE IS A FAIRY TALE WRITTEN BY GOD'S FINGERS.

Hans Christian Andersen

THE REAL SECRET OF HAPPINESS IS NOT WHAT YOU GIVE OR WHAT YOU RECEIVE; IT'S WHAT YOU SHARE.

ONE OF THE SECRETS
OF A HAPPY LIFE IS
CONTINUOUS SMALL
TREATS.

Iris Murdoch

IT IS, AFTER ALL, MOSTLY
LITTLE, COMMON THINGS
THAT MAKE UP OUR LIVES.

Elisabeth Elliot

REACH HIGH, FOR
STARS LIE HIDDEN IN
YOUR SOUL.

Pamela Vaull Starr

IDEALS MAY BE BEYOND
OUR REACH BUT
NEVER BEYOND OUR
FONDEST HOPES.

EVERY DAY IS A BIRTHDAY;
EVERY MOMENT OF It
IS NEW TO US; WE ARE
BORN AGAIN, RENEWED
FOR FRESH WORK AND
ENDEAVOR.

Isaac Watts

OH! LIFE IS SO FULL
AND RICH.

Pearl Bailey

MAY YOU LIVE AS LONG
AS YOU WANT AND
NOT WANT AS LONG
AS YOU LIVE.

Tom Hanks

THE NUMBER OF PEOPLE
WATCHING YOU IS
DIRECTLY PROPORTIONAL
TO THE SHADE OF
CRIMSON IN YOUR CHEEKS.

KEEP A SMILE ON THAT
WONDERFUL FACE OF
YOURS. AND BE HAPPY.

Collin Marty

TRUE FRIENDS INSPIRE
YOU TO BELIEVE THE BEST
IN YOURSELF, TO KEEP
PURSUING YOUR DEEPEST
DREAMS—AND MOST
WONDERFUL OF ALL, THEY
CELEBRATE YOUR JOYS AS
IF THEY WERE THEIR OWN.

I WISH YOU LONG LIFE
AND HAPPINESS—FOR YOUR
LONG LIFE WILL BE MY
HAPPINESS!

GOD'S BRIGHT SUNSHINE
OVERHEAD, GOD'S FLOWERS
BESIDE YOUR FEET...
AND BY SUCH PLEASANT
PATHWAYS LED,
MAY ALL YOUR LIFE
BE SWEET.

Helen Waithma

MAY YOUR HOURS OF
REMINISCENCE BE FILLED
WITH DAYS OF GOOD
CHEER AND WEEKS OF
PLEASANT MEMORIES.

I THANK MY GOD EVERY
TIME I REMEMBER YOU.

The Book of Philippians

THOSE WHO BRING
SUNSHINE TO THE LIVES
OF OTHERS CANNOT KEEP
IT FROM THEMSELVES.

Sir James M. Barrie

ALWAYS LAUGH WHEN YOU
CAN. MERRIMENT IS THE
SUNNY SIDE OF EXISTENCE.

Lord Byron

KEEP YOUR EYES ON THE
STARS AND YOUR FEET
ON THE GROUND.

Theodore Roosevelt

TODAY'S BRIGHT MOMENTS
ARE TOMORROW'S FOND
MEMORIES.

SOME

PEOPLE MAKE

THE WORLD SPECIAL

JUST BY BEING IN IT.

DANCE LIKE NO ONE
    IS WATCHING,
LOVE LIKE YOU'LL NEVER
    BE HURT,
SING LIKE NO ONE
    IS LISTENING,
LIVE LIKE IT'S HEAVEN
    ON EARTH.

William Purkey

THE GREATEST GIFT IS A PORTION OF YOURSELF.

Ralph Waldo Emerson

FOLLOW YOUR DREAM. IT IS COURAGEOUS TO LET YOUR HEART LEAD THE WAY.

Leland Thomas

WHEN YOU'VE GOT IT,
FLAUNT IT!

Zero Moste

IT IS FAR MORE
IMPRESSIVE WHEN OTHERS
DISCOVER YOUR GOOD
QUALITIES WITHOUT
YOUR HELP.

THERE IS NOTHING
ABOUT YOU MORE
MAGNETIC OR ATTRACTIVE
THAN YOUR SMILE.

Charles R. Swindoll

WHENEVER I THINK OF
YOU, I SMILE INSIDE!

WE ARE ALL HERE FOR A SPELL, GET ALL THE GOOD LAUGHS YOU CAN.

Will Rogers

A GOOD TIME TO LAUGH IS ANY TIME YOU CAN.

Linda Ellerbee

THERE IS SOMETHING
IN EVERY SEASON, IN
EVERY DAY, TO CELEBRATE.

Gloria Gaither

IT ISN'T THE BIG
PLEASURES THAT COUNT
THE MOST; IT'S MAKING A
GREAT DEAL OUT OF THE
LITTLE ONES.

Jean Webster

HOLD FAST YOUR DREAMS!
WITHIN YOUR HEART
KEEP ONE STILL,
   SECRET SPOT
WHERE DREAMS MAY GO
AND, SHELTERED SO,
MAY THRIVE AND GROW.

Louise Driscoll

MOST NEW DISCOVERIES
ARE SUDDENLY-SEEN
THINGS THAT WERE
ALWAYS THERE.

Susanne K. Langer

ALWAYS TAKE YOUR
RAINBOWS WITH YOU!

YOU DESERVE WISHES
GALORE AND DREAMS
THAT COME TRUE MORE
AND MORE!

YOUR ONLY TREASURES
ARE THOSE WHICH YOU
CARRY IN YOUR HEART.

Demophilus

RECALL IT AS OFTEN AS
YOU WISH, A HAPPY
MEMORY NEVER
WEARS OUT.

Libbie Fudim

MAY YOU LIVE ALL THE
DAYS OF YOUR LIFE.

Jonathan Swift

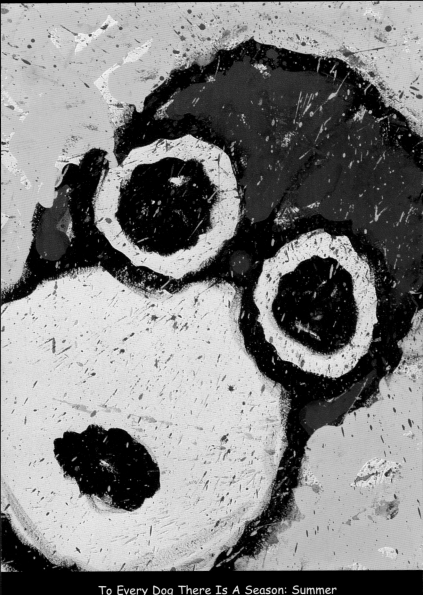

To Every Dog There Is A Season: Summer

ALWAYS

REMEMBER YOU'RE UNIQUE, JUST LIKE EVERYONE ELSE.

SPECIAL DAYS
SEND ME FLYING
ON YOUR SPECIAL DAY

Bright, expressive paintings by Tom Everhart,
the only artist authorized by Charles Schulz
to illustrate Peanuts characters, are paired with
lighthearted, fun-loving sentiments in this celebration
of birthdays and other momentous occasions.

Artwork copyright © 1999 UFS
Design by Lecy Design
Text copyright © 1999 FrontPorch Books,
a division of Garborg's, LLC

Published by Garborg's, LLC
P. O. Box 20132, Bloomington, MN 55420

ISBN 1-58375-467-9

Printed in Mexico